Keep this pocket-sized Frith book with you when you are visiting Suffolk, or if you are on holiday in the locality.

Whether you are in your car or on foot, you will enjoy an evocative journey back in time. Compare the Suffolk of old with what you can see today—see how the streets have changed; examine the shops and buildings and notice how they have been altered or replaced; look at fine details such as lamp-posts, shop fascias and trade signs; and see the many alterations to the Suffolk landscape that have taken place unnoticed during our lives, some of which we may have taken for granted.

At the turn of a page you will gain fascinating insights into Suffolk's unique history.

FRANCIS FRITH'S
pocket ALBUM

SUFFOLK

A POCKET ALBUM

Adapted from an original book by
CLIVE TULLY

First published in the United Kingdom in 2005 by
Frith Book Company Ltd

ISBN 1-85937-947-8

British Library Cataloguing in Publication Data

Suffolk—A Pocket Album
Adapted from an original book by Clive Tully

Frith Book Company Ltd
Frith's Barn, Teffont,
Salisbury, Wiltshire SP3 5QP
Tel: +44 (0) 1722 716 376
Email: info@francisfrith.co.uk
www.francisfrith.co.uk

Printed and bound in Great Britain by MPG, Bodmin

Front Cover: **SAXMUNDHAM**, The Village 1929   82947t
The colour-tinting is for illustrative purposes only, and is not intended to be historically accurate.

Frontispiece: **BLYTHBURGH**, the church and village 1895   36881

AS WITH ANY HISTORICAL DATABASE THE FRITH ARCHIVE IS CONSTANTLY
BEING CORRECTED AND IMPROVED AND THE PUBLISHERS WOULD WELCOME
INFORMATION ON OMISSIONS OR INACCURACIES

MILDENHALL, MARKET PLACE C1955 / M75011

CONTENTS

FRANCIS FRITH
VICTORIAN PIONEER

Francis Frith, founder of the world-famous photographic archive, was a complex and multi-talented man. A devout Quaker and a highly successful Victorian businessman, he was philosophic by nature and pioneering in outlook. By 1855 he had already established a wholesale grocery business in Liverpool, and sold it for the astonishing sum of £200,000, which is the equivalent today of over £15,000,000. Now in his thirties, and captivated by the new science of photography, Frith set out on a series of pioneering journeys up the Nile and to the Near East.

INTRIGUE AND EXPLORATION

He was the first photographer to venture beyond the sixth cataract of the Nile. Africa was still the mysterious 'Dark Continent', and Stanley and Livingstone's historic meeting was a decade into the future. The conditions for picture taking confound belief. He laboured for hours in his wicker dark-room in the sweltering heat of the desert, while the volatile chemicals fizzed dangerously in their trays. Back in London he exhibited his photographs and was 'rapturously cheered' by members of the Royal Society. His reputation as a photographer was made overnight.

VENTURE OF A LIFE-TIME

By the 1870s the railways had threaded their way across the country, and Bank Holidays and half-day Saturdays had been made obligatory by Act of Parliament. All of a sudden the working man and his family were able to enjoy days out, take holidays, and see a little more of the world.

With typical business acumen, Francis Frith foresaw that these new tourists would enjoy having souvenirs to commemorate their days out. For the next thirty years he travelled the country by train and by pony and trap, producing fine photographs of seaside resorts and beauty spots that were keenly bought by millions of Victorians. These prints were painstakingly pasted into family albums and pored over during the dark nights of winter, rekindling precious memories of summer excursions. Frith's studio was soon supplying retail shops all over the country, and by 1890 F Frith & Co had become the greatest specialist photographic publishing company in the world, with over 2,000 sales outlets, and pioneered the picture postcard.

FRANCIS FRITH'S LEGACY

Francis Frith had died in 1898 at his villa in Cannes, his great project still growing. The archive he created continued in business for another seventy years. By 1970 it contained over a third of a million pictures showing 7,000 British towns and villages.

Frith's legacy to us today is of immense significance and value, for the magnificent archive of evocative photographs he created provides a unique record of change in the cities, towns and villages throughout Britain over a century and more. Frith and his fellow studio photographers revisited locations many times down the years to update their views, compiling for us an enthralling and colourful pageant of British life and character.

We are fortunate that Frith was dedicated to recording the minutiae of everyday life. For it is this sheer wealth of visual data, the painstaking chronicle of changes in dress, transport, street layouts, buildings, housing, engineering and landscape that captivates us so much today, offering us a powerful link with the past and with the lives of our ancestors.

Computers have now made it possible for Frith's many thousands of images to be accessed almost instantly. The archive offers every one of us an opportunity to examine the places where we and our families have lived and worked down the years. Its images, depicting our shared past, are now bringing pleasure and enlightenment to millions around the world a century and more after his death.

SUFFOLK
AN INTRODUCTION

TO MANY, Suffolk might bring to mind the characterful colour-washed timber-framed houses of places like Lavenham or Kersey, or the soaring splendour of its churches. To others it might be that unique quality of light found on the coast at places like Southwold, and at Aldeburgh, which so inspired the composer Benjamin Britten. Along the coast, Walberswick proved a magnet to a whole host of distinguished artists, such as Charles Rennie Mackintosh and Stanley Spencer.

With Norfolk to the north, Essex to the south and Cambridgeshire to the west, Suffolk occupies the middle part of that distinctive bulge in the east coast of Britain. The boundaries are fairly straightforward topographically speaking. To the north, the boundary is the rivers Waveney and Little Ouse, to the south, the River Stour, while in the west, it is largely where the more rolling Suffolk countryside meets the flat fens of Cambridgeshire.

Suffolk has some fifty miles of coastline, much of it with beautiful heaths as its hinterland. Over the centuries, the shape of the coastline has changed considerably. Towns like Aldeburgh, Dunwich and Covehithe have all suffered from erosion. It is hard to imagine that the tiny hamlet that remains of Dunwich is but a tiny part of what was once one of the country's major ports. Elsewhere, the coastline has built up: Orford, for example, was once open to the sea, and is now separated from it by a long spit of shingle which formed due to a process called longshore drift. Generally, the fact that Suffolk's coastline is all low-lying has put it at risk from tidal surges – the worst being the 1953 floods which affected much of the East Coast.

Just over 900 years ago, at the time of the Domesday Survey of 1086, Suffolk was one of the most densely populated areas in the country. There were just a few large towns, but over 400 villages. William rewarded various nobles who had helped him with the conquest by awarding them numerous manors. Three powerful families had the lion's share of Suffolk between them, but by the middle of the 12th century, it was the ambitious Bigod family who controlled the county. Henry II countered the threat by building the castle at Orford, and attacking Framlingham castle.

Between the time of the conquest and Henry VIII, it was the religious orders who held sway. They became the landowners, imposing not just rents on their tenants, but taxes as well. It was the provocation of such taxes that led to the abbey of St Edmundsbury being burned down in 1327. In the 13th century, many English barons believed in certain principles of government, drawing up a charter which they wanted King John to ratify. On the 20th November 1214, they met at Bury St Edmunds abbey church in secret, and swore an oath to compel the king to sign, by force if necessary. As twenty-five barons secretly plotting against the king might not be favourably regarded in some quarters, it was logical that they should choose to meet here, at an important place of pilgrimage, where they hoped that their assembly would go unnoticed. The king signed the following year, at

Runnymede, and the Magna Carta has formed the basis of government of this country ever since.

Over the centuries, a number of different industries have kept Suffolk prosperous. In medieval times, the backbone of industry in the area was the wool and cloth-weaving trade. Many Dutch and Flemish weavers settled here when sheep farming was at its height, and created a wool industry which became world-famous. As a result, many buildings in East Anglia have a pronounced Dutch influence. At the peak of the industry, Suffolk was producing more wool than any other county in England, with various local variations of heavy broadcloth (the best known came from Kersey) exported all over Europe. By the reign of Elizabeth I, however, heavy broadcloths had gone out of fashion, replaced by lighter and more colourful fabrics. While Sudbury managed to adapt and turn out fine silks, many Suffolk towns lost the opportunity to adapt to the changing circumstances. When the first power looms were invented - devices relying on fast running water to provide the power - the textile industry moved north to the Pennines, and when coal became the fuel for industry in the 19th century, the textile factories were already well placed to utilise it.

Suffolk had a thriving fishing industry as well; the herring trade in particular made the fortunes of several coastal towns. But the changing shape of the coastline played its part, too. As medieval ports silted up, so the fishermen turned to other forms of fishing. Lowestoft retained its importance as a fishing port, although latter years have seen a decline due to European fishing quotas.

Agriculture has always been a part of the Suffolk landscape, and there were times in history when it was doubtless very profitable, evidenced by some of the huge brick barns which can still be found around the county, even if most have been converted into characterful dwellings in the recent years. Suffolk's rich pastures proved good for grazing cattle and sheep, and the abundance of oak forests meant that there was plenty of oak bark, an essential component of tanning. So it was that many Suffolk towns profited from the leather industry, which shipped goods as far away as India.

The coming of the railway in the 19th century undoubtedly changed the face of the region. Although the sailing barges which carried goods up and down the east coast carried on into the early 20th century, the trains started to eat into their business. But the biggest changes came simply with the movement of people. Towns like Lowestoft and Felixstowe became tourist resorts, and many developments followed rapidly.

Churches in Suffolk give a fascinating insight into the past, and the people who built them. Many villages and towns celebrated their prosperity from wool in this way (building and decorating their churches undoubtedly eased their consciences), but others were paid for by the profits from fishing, plundering and military gains. The majority of Suffolk churches date from the mid-14th to the 15th century, the Perpendicular period, with contrasting stone and patterned flint

BURY ST EDMUNDS, CORNHILL 1898 / 41246

flushwork. The churches were decorated lavishly inside, too, with wall paintings illustrating religious themes. But the most brightly decorated objects, the rood screens built across the naves of many churches, fell victim to Henry VIII's ban on such objects of veneration. The greatest Puritanism came during the Cromwellian period, when walls were whitewashed, and all kinds of ornamentation was damaged. The last major period of change came in Victorian times, when many churches were 'restored'. Thatched naves were roofed in slate, old style box pews were replaced, and organs came into general use.

Many of Suffolk's most famous inhabitants have come from the arts - poets, painters, or musicians. George Crabbe is probably the county's most distinguished poet, who was born in Aldeburgh in 1754. His poem about the embittered fisherman Peter Grimes inspired an opera by a much later and better known resident, Benjamin Britten.

The first Aldeburgh Festival came about in 1948, founded by Britten, the singer Peter Pears, and Eric Crozier. They decided to set up a modest festival, initially held in Aldeburgh's Jubilee Hall, and various

FELIXSTOWE, FROM THE BEACH 1899 / 44513

churches in the area. The festival's popularity grew to the point where a permanent home for the festival was founded at Snape Maltings.

It was Aldeburgh, too, that was home to Elizabeth Garrett Anderson, the first woman Doctor of Medicine, and founder of a hospital in London. She also became the first woman mayor of an English Borough when she took up office in Aldeburgh in 1908.

Thomas Gainsborough worked in Bath, and later London, but it was in Suffolk where he was born and brought up. The house in Sudbury where Gainsborough was born, formerly a 16th century inn, is now preserved as a museum and exhibition gallery, and it is the only artist's birthplace open to the public in the country. While Gainsborough loved to paint landscapes, it was the informality and grace of his portraits which won him far-reaching acclaim.

But of course Suffolk's best known painter is also one of Britain's – John Constable, who was born in 1776. His father, Golding, a miller, owned mills at Dedham and Flatford, and two windmills at East Bergholt. Golding wanted him to follow in the family business, but with encouragement from his mother, John went to London to study art, eventually gaining a place at the Royal Academy. Although his early commissions were not to his own taste, he persevered with painting the countryside where he was brought up around Dedham Vale, in a style which at the time was not generally acceptable. When 'The Hay Wain' was first shown in the Royal Academy in 1818, it received a response which was luke-warm, to say the least. In Paris, where impressionist painting had already taken off, he was feted as a celebrity, and was awarded a gold medal by the King of France. His work only received recognition at home later on.

Somerleyton Hall dates back to Elizabethan times, although it was extensively rebuilt in 1846 by Sir Samuel Morton Peto, who made his fortune out of the railways. The mansion has some lavishly furnished state rooms, and the gardens include a maze.

SOMERLEYTON HALL

1891 / 28725

Somerleyton Hall's impressive cast iron and glass-domed winter garden, with its rich abundance of ferns, climbing plants and typical Victorian ornamentation. It was demolished in 1914.

SOMERLEYTON HALL

1891 / 28730

A sailing vessel negotiates the harbour entrance. This is where busy port and tourism came together. The South Pier, which forms the southern part of the harbour, and from where this picture was taken, was a popular stroll for holidaymakers.

LOWESTOFT
ENTRANCE TO THE HARBOUR

1887 / 19838

LOWESTOFT, THE BEACH

1887 / 19886

A typical late Victorian beach scene, with donkey rides, a complete absence of skin exposed to the sun, and a photographer's equipment - a tripod and a cart for storing the glass plates - to the left of the picture.

LOWESTOFT, CONVALESCENT HOME

1887 / 19856

LOWESTOFT
LONDON ROAD

1896 / 37924

Here we see solid Victorian architecture in this tree-lined street, with one well-established family retail chain much in evidence. Lowestoft is very much a mixture of fishing port and seaside resort, the latter the result of the arrival of the railway in the mid 19th century.

LOWESTOFT
SOUTH PIER PAVILION

1896 / 37937

The iron-framed Pier Pavilion can be seen in the background. The growth of Lowestoft in Victorian times was largely down to construction by the civil engineer Samuel Morton Peto, who lived in the splendid Somerleyton Hall nearby. He was also involved with the building of Nelson's Column, the Houses of Parliament, and railway lines the world over.

LOWESTOFT
THE YACHT BASIN

1896 / 37939

The changeover from sail to steam saw a resurgence in business for the port of Lowestoft. This photograph of the High Lighthouse was taken at a time when the Great War, which saw the use of tanks like this one, was still very much in recent memory.

LOWESTOFT
THE HIGH LIGHTHOUSE

1921 / 71705

Holidaymakers enjoy a bracing walk as the waves crash up against the sea wall. From the amount of spray being kicked up in the distance, it's a fair bet that somebody got wet!

This is St Andrews church and the ruins of the former nave. The original church was left in ruins after the Civil War, and the smaller replacement was built within the ruins, its tower a useful navigational aid for mariners offshore. The ruins were the subject of a watercolour by the artist John Sell Cotman in 1804.

COVEHITHE
THE CHURCH AND RUINS

1892 / 29930

Just north of the village is Brewery House, home of Sir William Hooker and his son Joseph. Not satisfied with the family business of brewing, they left to travel the world collecting plants, and eventually founded Kew Gardens.

HALESWORTH
MARKET PLACE

c1955 / H384019

HALESWORTH
THE THOROUGHFARE

c1955 / H384005

The Thoroughfare is Halesworth's main shopping street. In the mid 18th century, improvements in navigation on the River Blyth led to a big improvement in trade for the area's maltsters and brewers.

Blythburgh was an important port in bygone times. In the same way as many other river ports, it lost trade when its waterways could no longer cope with the increasing draughts of cargo ships. The church, known locally as 'the cathedral of the marshes', with its 128ft nave and 83ft tower, presents an imposing landmark. It was over this church that a Liberator bomber exploded in August 1944, killing Joseph Kennedy, eldest brother of the late US president.

BLYTHBURGH
THE CHURCH

1895 / 36879

SOUTHWOLD
HIGH STREET

1892 / 29926

Broad pavements and a dirt road characterise this turn-of-the-century view. These days, the renowned Crown Hotel presents less of a stark exterior, with a lighter colour scheme, and potted plants and shrubs.

Close to the point where the cliffs begin to rise from the beach at Southwold is the Sailor's Reading Room. It was founded in 1864 by a naval widow, whose intentions were 'to wean the fishermen from their alleged failings - going to sea on the Sabbath, and getting drunk on any day of the week'. The beach itself is dotted with numerous fishing boats.

SOUTHWOLD

1893 / 32182

Looming over the rooftops is the gleaming white tower of the lighthouse, built just six years previously. These days, East Green is perhaps best known as the Mecca for all local beer drinkers - Adnams Brewery!

SOUTHWOLD
EAST GREEN

1893 / 32184

While many houses burned down in the fire of 1659, the 15th century church of St. Edmund survived because the churchyard served as a fire break.

SOUTHWOLD FROM THE LIGHTHOUSE

1893 / 32186

In 1659, Southwold suffered a huge fire which destroyed a substantial part of the town. The rebuilding which followed left nine greens - effective firebreaks against any future catastrophe - and it is these which give Southwold its unique character.

SOUTHWOLD
THE GREEN

1896 / 38624

SOUTHWOLD
THE BEACH

1896 / 38620

The beach is lined with numerous beach yawls; these did all the fetching and carrying for the cargo-carrying ships which plied the North Sea, as well as competing for lucrative salvage prizes when they foundered. Double-ended clinker-built boats with twin lugsails, they were capable of sailing at speed, an essential prerequisite for the job.

It must have been a hot day when this photograph was taken - note the boaters, the parasol and the baby in a frilly sunbonnet enjoying a ride in a goatcart. The market still takes place here today.

SOUTHWOLD THE MARKET

1896 / 38627

A typical beach scene, in an age when modesty was paramount. Ladies would take to the water from the bathing machines rolled down to water's edge. The holidaymakers in the deck chairs on the beach will be 'taking the air' rather than working on suntans - a tanned skin would not become fashionable until the 1920s.

SOUTHWOLD
FROM THE PIER

1906 / 56829

The centre of the Market Place is marked by a splendid Victorian cast
iron water pump, decorated with fish, crown and arrows, and the motto
'Defend They Ryghts'. The Swan Hotel is mainly Georgian, with
Edwardian bays added on. Note the elegant wrought ironwork above
the sign.

SOUTHWOLD
MARKET PLACE

1919 / 69121

This couple passing the time of day, or maybe waiting for the ferry to take them across the river to Southwold, are on the bank of the River Blyth.

WALBERSWICK
THE RIVER BANK

1892 / 29933

This chain ferry across the River Blyth from Walberswick to Southwold was operated by the River Blyth Ferry Company. Started up in 1885, the original hand-cranked ferry was later replaced by one which was steam-powered.

WALBERSWICK
THE FERRY

1919 / 69127

A quaint wooden footbridge gives this pedestrian relatively quick access over the River Blyth where it is joined by Buss Creek to Southwold. Horsedrawn carriages and motorised vehicles had to take a much longer route, about nine miles, via Blythburgh.

WALBERSWICK
THE BRIDGE

1919 / 69129

43

WALBERSWICK
THE VILLAGE

1919 / 69128

Not much more than St James's Street is left of Dunwich, once the seat of the Saxon king of East Anglia, and once one of the greatest and most prosperous ports in the country. When this picture was taken, what remained of Dunwich still had the last of its old churches. It had started to collapse five years previously, and finally fell into the sea in 1918.

DUNWICH
THE VILLAGE

1909 / 62043

North of Saxmundham, Yoxford was once a coaching stop on the London to Great Yarmouth route. Outside St Peter's church, an ornate cast iron signpost erected in 1830 has hands pointing to London, Yarmouth and Framlingham. The business of taking a photograph is still sufficiently unusual to ensure the subjects do not act naturally, and inevitably one of the boys has failed to heed the photographer's pleas to keep still for the duration of the exposure!

YOXFORD
THE VILLAGE

1909 / 62051

SAXMUNDHAM

1929 / 82948

SAXMUNDHAM
HIGH STREET

1929 / 82947

Saxmundham saw a good deal of change when the railway arrived in the 19th century. The Bell Hotel was built in 1842.

There's a delightfully pensive look on the face of the little girl in this picture. Did the photographer capture a genuine moment, or was she posed? On the other side of the street, well-known shoe retailers Freeman, Hardy and Willis announce the best bargains since the beginning of the Great War.

LEISTON SIZEWELL ROAD

1922 / 72579

51

North of Leiston are the flint and brick ruins of the 14th-century Leiston Abbey. Of the church, only the Lady Chapel remains as a complete building, a result of its usefulness for storing grain after the Dissolution.

LEISTON
THE ABBEY

1894 / 33370

LEISTON
HIGH STREET

1922 / 72577

The headline on the newsagent's billboard refers to the continuing turmoil that followed the end of World War I and the Treaty of Versailles, and the Germans' obligation to pay reparations.

Here we are overlooking the beach, the upper part populated by marram or 'bentgrass'. As a holiday village, what we see here has to be one of the first examples of parking problems anywhere!

THORPENESS
THE BENTHILLS

1929 / 82979

The curious 'House in the Clouds' is in fact a water tower. The upper part conceals the tank, while the creosoted portion below provides living accommodation. The post mill in the foreground originally ground corn at Aldringham, but was moved to its present position in the 1920s to pump water into the 'House in the Clouds'.

THORPENESS
THE HOUSE IN THE
CLOUDS AND THE MILL

c1955 / T38012

In 1862, an important archaeological find was made half a mile east from here. A Saxon ship burial was discovered, 48 feet long. It has since been dated to between AD635 and 650.

SNAPE
THE CHURCH

1909 / 62024

Holidaymakers enjoy a stroll along the Parade.
In the distance is a lookout tower, one of two.
While there are recreational activities available
on the beach, it is very much a working one,
evidenced by the yawls on the shingle.

ALDEBURGH
THE ESPLANADE

1896 / 38668

The timber-framed Tudor Moot Hall is situated next to the beach. When it was built, the meeting house was actually right in the centre of town, but coastal erosion over hundreds of years has swept away much of the old town, and left the beach almost next door to the building.

ALDEBURGH
THE MOOT HALL

1894 / 33360

*The High Street is Aldeburgh's main area of activity, and
from here the Town Steps lead off up a steep hill. Here
grand houses enjoy a superb view overlooking the town and
coastline below.*

ALDEBURGH
THE STEPS

1906 / 56826

The poet George Crabbe was born in Aldeburgh in 1754. His poem about the embittered fisherman Peter Grimes inspired an opera by a much later and better known resident, Benjamin Britten. Just 14 years after this photograph was taken, Elizabeth Garrett Anderson, the first woman Doctor of Medicine, became first woman mayor of an English borough when she took up office in Aldeburgh in 1908.

ALDEBURGH
OLD MARKET SQUARE

1929 / 82976

ALDEBURGH
HIGH STREET
1894 / 33362

The broad High Street is mainly Victorian, peppered with Georgian buildings. The original Tudor town plan was based on a series of both parallel and converging streets, but erosion during the 17th and 18th centuries resulted in many houses being lost to the sea.

A tranquil scene in the quiet little village of Bawdsey. Some thirty years later, Bawdsey was to play a vital part in the defence of Britain against the Luftwaffe. This is where the scientist Robert Watson-Watt developed radar, and indeed, here too was one of the five strategic radar stations situated along the coast between Bawdsey and Dover.

BAWDSEY
THE VILLAGE GREEN

1907 / 58988

Henry II's great 12th-century keep stands sentinel over Orford, built to guard the coast where Flemish mercenaries were brought ashore by the Earl of Norfolk, whose castles far out-numbered royal castles in East Anglia. It was the first to be built with a keep which is cylindrical inside and polygonal outside, reinforced by three projecting rectangular turrets.

ORFORD
THE VILLAGE

1909 / 62017

The Bell Inn (now the Bell and Steelyard) stands in New Street. The covered hoist is a steelyard, used for weighing grain wagons from the early 17th century to the 1880s. Capable of weighing up to 2.5 tons, it would weigh the wagon before going to market, and again when it returned empty. No doubt the day's trade would be celebrated over a pint in the inn!

WOODBRIDGE
THE BELL INN

1894 / 33375

Although quite narrow and winding, this is the main street of the town, stretching for nearly a mile, and running parallel with the River Deben.

WOODBRIDGE
THE THOROUGHFARE

1894 / 33374

At the bottom of the picture is the Bull Hotel, host to Alfred Lord Tennyson in 1876, when he was Poet Laureate. Another well-known poet lived nearby - Edward Fitzgerald, who translated the Rubaiyat of Omar Khayyam.

WOODBRIDGE FROM THE CHURCH TOWER
1894 / 33984

This view looks along Church Street at its junction with Cumberland Street (left) and the Thoroughfare (right). The Cross Public House, according to its sign established in 1652, almost certainly took its name from its position on the crossroads.

WOODBRIDGE
CHURCH STREET

1906 / 53497

FELIXSTOWE
FROM THE BEACH

1899 / 44513

No shortage of holidaymakers on the beach at turn-of-the-century Felixstowe. The only shortage here, a hundred years ago, is that of exposed skin. This was an era when modesty prevailed.

Capturing a street scene on film was not as easy a hundred years ago as it is now. But despite the fact that the relatively long exposure has meant that the moving people have blurred, the resulting photograph conveys a natural feel that is lacking in so many posed scenes of the same era.

FELIXSTOWE
BANK CORNER

1899 / 44519

WALTON
HIGH STREET

1899 / 43246

At this time, Felixstowe enjoyed popularity as a seaside resort, but the dream of eccentric local landowner Colonel Tomline to transform the town into a major port had not yet materialised - that was to take another fifty years! Here, in Walton High Street, the occasional pony and trap seems to be the only contribution to heavy traffic.

At the turn of the century, Felixstowe was at the height of its popularity as a seaside resort, with its south-facing beach. Of course, in Edwardian times bathing machines were very much the order of the day, and even on the beach a strict sense of decorum was maintained.

FELIXSTOWE
THE BEACH

1904 / 51254

At this time, Felixstowe was a genteel seaside resort, with steamers pulling up at the pier with passengers from Great Yarmouth, Walton-on-the-Naze, Clacton, and even London. Perhaps the most interesting thing about this photograph is the parked car on the right. Closer examination reveals that in fact the car was pasted over the original print - common practice at the time to bring photographs up to date.

FELIXSTOWE
THE PIER

1906 / 54640

PIN MILL

1909 / 62001A

It was local landowner Colonel Tomline who promoted a railway and a new dock in Felixstowe, in the hope of being able to compete with the port of Harwich across the Orwell Estuary. The dock did not succeed until well after his death, but the railway meantime stimulated the development of Felixstowe as a seaside resort.

FELIXSTOWE
THE DOCKS

1907 / 58986

The 97 feet high tower of St Michael's church dominates this view of Beccles, seen from the River Waveney. Wherries were still used to transport heavy goods, such as the timber seen here.

BECCLES
THE RIVER BRIDGE
1894 / 33331

The Market Square of Beccles is overlooked by the detached
tower of St Michael's church. The building on the left was
home to the offices of the East Suffolk Gazette, with the
ground floor taken up as a shop.

BECCLES
MARKET SQUARE

1900 / 45096

79

Sixty years on, Beccles has declined as a port, with goods being carried more by road. The church is unusual in that the 92 feet high tower is actually separate from the nave.

BECCLES
NEW MARKET
c1955 / B45045

In the days when Bungay was a thriving port, trading wherries would come through Geldeston Lock near Beccles, and sail up the Waveney to what used to be the limit of navigation for large craft. Later on, the Waveney became limited to small pleasure boats, such as this rowing boat seen on a tranquil stretch of the river.

BUNGAY
RIVER WAVENEY
c1955 / B617002

A year after a fire razed most of Bungay to the ground in 1688, the Butter Cross was built to commemorate it. It is a pretty octagonal building with a dome surmounted by a figure of Justice; a cage underneath was used to hold the local felons to public ridicule, although by the time this photograph was taken, it was no longer in service! The board standing up against one of the pillars is offering a circular tour of Southwold and Lowestoft.

BUNGAY
MARKET PLACE

1951 / B617026

Tables and chairs are ready in a relaxing riverside setting. Barges once travelled up the Little Ouse as far as Brandon and Thetford, although here it is much more the province of pleasure boaters.

BRANDON
THE RIVER OUSE

1925 / 78270

Brandon's market has been in existence for over 650 years. The town was once the centre of flint-knapping, at its height during the Napoleonic wars, employing two hundred men producing gunflints.

BRANDON
MARKET PLACE

1925 / 78271A

IPSWICH
THE BUTTER MARKET

1893 / 32204

On the corner with St Stephens Lane stands the Ancient House, a remarkable building which is probably the best surviving example of medieval pargetting - decorative plasterwork - in Britain.

When this photograph was taken, the richly pargetted Ancient House, which dates back to medieval times, was occupied by Fred Pawsey, selling books and stationery.

IPSWICH
THE ANCIENT HOUSE

1893 / 32205

IPSWICH
ST STEPHENS LANE

1921 / 70391

IPSWICH
THE BUTTER MARKET

1921 / 70404

Up until 1810, Ipswich's Butter Market was indeed the scene for the sale of butter and other products. At this time, it is one of the main shopping streets in the town. At the far end on the left is the Ancient House, with its unmistakable overhanging upper storey.

A sailing barge negotiates the lock gates. The Wet Dock was constructed in Ipswich between 1839 and 1842, and at the time it was the most revolutionary and the biggest of its kind in the country.

IPSWICH
THE LOCK GATES

1921 / 70413

IPSWICH
ST PETERS DOCK

1921 / 70411

Sailing barges tied up in the Wet Dock, the non-tidal part of the port of Ipswich. Adjacent to the dock are large warehouses, including that of Cranfields, who along with Pauls, owned their own large fleets of barges.

The castle was built in 1190 by the famous Bigod family, and was one of the first castles not to include a keep. Instead, it has thirteen separate towers, linked by a curtain wall, a Saracen idea brought back by returning Crusaders. It was at Framlingham in 1553 that Mary Tudor organised her army of supporters to march on Lady Jane Grey, and here, later, she proclaimed herself Queen.

FRAMLINGHAM
THE CASTLE

1909 / 62032

The war memorial, clock tower and telephone box grace
the Square. In the church nearby is a memorial to Captain
Edward Rotherham, who commanded a ship of the line, the
'Royal Sovereign', at the Battle of Trafalgar.

BILDESTON
THE SQUARE
c1960 / B766021

These are 17th-century buildings. The Coffee Tavern came into being around thirty years previously - in an attempt to provide people with an alternative to nearby public houses.

HADLEIGH
OLD HOUSES IN THE HIGH STREET

1922 / 71970

Looking in the opposite direction from the Coffee Tavern, this view of Hadleigh's High Street shows the George public house and, further down on the same side, the White Lion Hotel. The building in between has its upper storey decorated by pargetting - moulded plasterwork.

HADLEIGH
HIGH STREET

C1955 / H2007

In the distance is the church of St John the Baptist, once a chapel to nearby Barking. From the outside, the roof has an odd look about it, but inside, it is one of the most remarkable examples of a timber roof in East Anglia.

NEEDHAM MARKET HIGH STREET

1922 / 71933

The village school in Old Newton, just north of Stowmarket.
This was an era when every village had its school - now of
course, much consolidation has taken place.

OLD NEWTON
THE SCHOOL

c1955 / O97013

STOWMARKET
IPSWICH STREET

C1955 / S583007A

This quiet little village north of Woodbridge was granted a market in the mid 15th century by Henry VI. Four hundred years later, it was here that John Kirby wrote his influential 'Suffolk Traveller'.

WICKHAM MARKET
MARKET HILL

1929 / 82047

It was Flatford and nearby East Bergholt which provided the young John Constable with the inspiration for many of his fine paintings. Flatford Mill, built in 1733, featured in several of Constable's works. This thatched cottage is called, appropriately enough, Bridge Cottage.

FLATFORD
BRIDGE COTTAGE

1907 / 57552

This early 16th-century timber building was commissioned
by the Guild of Corpus Christi, a trade organisation which
regulated the local industry of wool production. The heavy
oak studwork - far more than is required for structural
stability - reflects the wealth of the wool trade.

LAVENHAM
THE GUILDHALL

1904 / 51180

103

Thatched roofs abound. While wheat straw is often used as the roofing material, the chances are that these houses will be thatched with longer-lasting reed from the Broads. The church and green were once the subject of railway posters promoting Suffolk.

MONK'S ELEIGH
THE STREET

c1955 / M270003

The red-brick Tudor manor house of Kentwell Hall stands at the northern end of Long Melford. Today it is best known for the striking Tudor Rose brickwork maze set into the courtyard.

LONG MELFORD
KENTWELL HALL

1895 / 35495

The Town Mill was built on the site of a Saxon mill. The youths sitting on the wall in front could be posing for the camera, or they might just be dangling a line into the mill stream to see what they might catch. In recent years, the building has been converted into a hotel, with the water wheel inside kept as a feature of the dining room.

SUDBURY
THE MILL
1895 / 35484

Market Hill is lined with elegant Georgian buildings, with
St Peter's church at the top. The artist Thomas Gainsborough
was born here in a former 16th-century inn, and he lived
and worked here for a number of years.

SUDBURY
THE MARKET

1904 / 51156

PAKENHAM
THE WINDMILL

c1955 / P286003

This enormous gate, originally built with defence in mind, once led into the monastery courtyard. It stands on the site of an earlier gateway, which had been destroyed by the townsfolk during an uprising against the harsh rule of the Abbey.

BURY ST EDMUNDS
THE ABBEY GATE

1922 / 71956

BURY ST EDMUNDS
CORNHILL

1898 / 41246

The original market place, as laid out in the Bury St Edmunds' grid pattern
devised by Abbot Baldwin in the 11th century, was a good deal larger than it
was by the time this photograph was taken. Market stalls became permanent
over the years, and ended up as two complete rows of buildings. Here, a few
street vendors have set out their stalls.

The 15th-century St Mary's church is the burial place of Mary Tudor, sister of Henry VIII, and noted for its decorated 'Angel Roof' nave. On the junction with Westgate Street is the Theatre Royal, one of only three surviving Regency theatres in the country, built in 1819 by National Gallery architect William Wilkins. The theatre is famous for its world premiere of 'Charley's Aunt' in 1892.

BURY ST EDMUNDS
CROWN STREET

1929 / 81935

*This photograph was taken back in the
days when an open space in a town did not
have to be completely covered by cars! The
Angel Hotel was immortalised in Dickens'
'Pickwick Papers'.*

BURY ST EDMUNDS
ANGEL HOTEL

1929 / 81945

The pretty little village of Barton Mills, and the Bull Inn. In the 13th century, the local rector, Jacobus de Scabellis, became a cardinal, and ultimately, Pope Honorius IV.

BARTON MILLS
THE BULL INN

1925 / 78288

Not something that would happen today with any degree of safety, a gentleman poses for the camera in the middle of the street. The timbered building on the left, occupied at the time by Barclays Bank, was originally built with plastered upper walls and gables, later exposed to give the building a mock Tudor flavour.

MILDENHALL
HIGH STREET

1925 / 78279

A small market town of medieval origin where the Fens meet Breckland, Mildenhall gained an airfield between the wars, the starting point for many famous air races. The airfield subsequently became a base for the United States Air Force (now the headquarters of the USAF in Europe). Here in the Market Place, the large car provides ample evidence of the American presence.

MILDENHALL MARKET PLACE

c1955 / M75008

MILDENHALL
HIGH STREET

c1965 / M75056

The church has a particularly fine ceiling decorated with angels. Just over twenty years previously, a farm worker had unearthed a hoard of Roman treasure - now displayed in the British Museum.

NEWMARKET
HIGH STREET

1929 / 81955

The High Street used to be the main Norwich to London road. Here is a foretaste of the traffic problems that were to come.

This is a daily sight around the capital of horse racing - stable lads exercising racehorses on Newmarket Heath.

NEWMARKET
HORSES AT EXERCISE

1922 / 71918

The old part of the town is mainly late Victorian, although it expanded rapidly after World War II as an overspill for London.

HAVERHILL HIGH STREET

c1955 / H381003

INDEX

PLEASE HELP US BRING FRITH'S PHOTOGRAPHS TO LIFE

Our authors do their best to recount the history of the places they write about. They give insights into how particular towns and villages developed, they describe the architecture of streets and buildings, and they discuss the lives of famous people who lived there. But however knowledgeable our authors are, the story they tell is necessarily incomplete.

Frith's photographs are so much more than plain historical documents. They are living proofs of the flow of human life down the generations. They show real people at real moments in history; and each of those people is the son or daughter of someone, the brother or sister, aunt or uncle, grandfather or grandmother of someone else. All of them lived, worked and played in the streets depicted in Frith's photographs.

We would be grateful if you would tell us about the many places shown in our photographs—the streets with their buildings, shops, businesses and industries. Describe your own memories of life in those streets: what it was like growing up there, who ran the local shop and what shopping was like years ago; if your workplace is shown tell us about your working day and what the building is used for now. With your help more and more Frith photographs can be brought to life, and vital memories preserved for posterity.

We will gradually add your comments and stories to the archive for the benefit of historians of the future. Wherever possible, we will try to include some of your comments in future editions of our books. Moreover, if you spot errors in dates, titles or other facts, please let us know, because our archive records are not always completely accurate—they rely on 150 years of human endeavour and hand-compiled records.

So please write, fax or email us with your stories and memories. Thank you!

FREE PRINT OF YOUR CHOICE

Choose any Frith photograph in this book.
Simply complete the Voucher opposite and
return it with your remittance for £2.25 (to
cover postage and handling) and we will print
the photograph of your choice in SEPIA (size
11 x 8 inches) and supply it in a cream mount
with a burgundy rule line
(overall size 14 x 11 inches).
**Please note: photographs with a reference number
starting with a "Z" are not Frith photographs and
cannot be supplied under this offer.**
Offer valid for delivery to UK one address only.

Mounted Print
Overall size 14 x 11 inches (355 x 280mm)

**PLUS: Order additional Mounted Prints at
HALF PRICE - £7.49 each** (normally £14.99)
If you would like to order more Frith prints
from this book, possibly as gifts for friends and
family, you can buy them at half price (with no
additional postage and handling costs).

PLUS: Have your Mounted Prints framed
For an extra £14.95 per print you can have your
mounted print(s) framed in an elegant polished
wood and gilt moulding, overall size
16 x 13 inches (no additional postage and
handling required).

IMPORTANT!

These special prices are only
available if you use this form to
order. You must use the ORIGINAL
VOUCHER (no copies permitted).

We can only despatch to one
UK address. This offer cannot be
combined with any other offer.

FRITH PRODUCTS AND SERVICES

All Frith photographs are available for you to buy as framed or mounted prints.
From time to time, other illustrated items such as Address Books and Maps are also
available. Already, almost 80,000 Frith archive photographs can be viewed and
purchased on the internet through the Frith website.

For more detailed information on Frith companies and products, visit:

www.francisfrith.co.uk

For further information, or trade enquiries, contact:

The Francis Frith Collection, Frith's Barn, Teffont, Salisbury SP3 5QP

Tel: +44 (0) 1722 716 376 Fax: +44 (0) 1722 716 881 Email: sales@francisfrith.co.uk

Voucher

for FREE and Reduced Price Frith Prints

Do not photocopy this voucher. Only the original is valid, so please fill it in, cut it out and return it to us with your order.

	Picture ref no	Page number	Qty	Mounted @ £7.49	Framed + £14.95	Orders Total £
1			1	Free of charge*	£	£
2				£7.49	£	£
3				£7.49	£	£
4				£7.49	£	£
5				£7.49	£	£
6				£7.49	£	£

Please allow 28 days for delivery. Offer available to one UK address only

* Post & handling	£2.25
Total Order Cost	£

Title of this book . . . .

I enclose a cheque / postal order for £ . . . .
payable to 'The Francis Frith Collection'

OR debit my Mastercard / Visa / Maestro / Amex card

Card Number

Issue No (Maestro only)   Valid from (Amex/Maestro)

Expires   Signature

Name Mr/Mrs/Ms . . . .
Address . . . .
. . . .
. . . .
. . . . .Postcode. . . . .
Daytime Tel No . . . .
E-mail . . . .

Valid to 31/12/07